M000019240

How to Help Your Child Succeed in School

A Parent's Guide to Helping Children Become Better Students

By
Debra Chapoton
B.A., M.A.T. Oakland University
and
Paul Chapoton
B.A., M.A.in Guidance & Counseling, Oakland University,
Ed. Spec. Wayne State University

ISBN: 9781795821285

© Copyright 2019 by Debra Chapoton All rights reserved.

Contents

1: Make a Homework

Schedule

A kid's job is to work at learning.

That's right. A kid's job is to learn.

Doing homework is a key factor in their success. Start a routine in the early grades and stick to it. Have a place where homework is to be done daily (kitchen or dining table, desk or counter, but not bed or floor) and keep an eye on things. There should be no excuses for not completing assignments. Teachers are not unreasonable tyrants.

Start a tradition even if your child doesn't receive regular homework assignments. That tradition might be that 4 pm until 5, Monday through Thursday, is set aside for homework, whether it is written work, reading, or studying. You can add Friday to this routine or switch it to Sunday afternoon if necessary. If work isn't finished by 5 pm then add an extra homework session after dinner.

Speaking of dinner, that's a good time to go over what happened at school each day. Families that eat dinner together reap additional rewards: kids' behavior is better, attitudes are less confrontational, adults are more informed about their kids' activities, and everyone in the family has a chance unload any stresses from the day.

What parents can do to help with homework:

1. Check the work.

2. Ask the child to explain it or teach the material to the parent.

3. Provide a quiet area to work and study.

4. Sit nearby and just be there.

5. Expect the work to be completed.

6. Check that the finished work gets back to school.

7. Ask to see the corrected work when it's returned.

Teacher tip:

If you have a student who consistently avoids turning in assignments, take the initiative and write up your own check list. For example, in the early grades you might send your child to school on Friday with a note like this:

Johnny has turned in all his work this week. Yes/No

Johnny is missing the following assignment(s)

_____

Teacher's signature_____

For older students you will have to make a more involved sheet. Something like this:

1st hour: missing assignments? _____

Teacher _____

2nd hour: missing assignments?_____

Teacher_____

[and so on for each class].

Don't worry that you're bothering the teacher. We
love parental involvement!

2: Support Your Child

Be involved in school.

Make involvement a priority.

Go to school open houses, conferences, plays, sports and anything else. Don't stop going when your kids get to high school, in fact, that is the time to be even more involved. One thing that good students have in common is backing from their parent(s).

Maybe you didn't have a positive school experience, but don't let your kid know that until they graduate. Say good things about education, stress the importance of reading and learning, and always support those in authority: teachers, coaches, and administrators.

What parents can do to be involved:

1. Join the parent/teacher organization.

2. Volunteer to help chaperon field trips.

3. Ask the teacher what else you can do to help out.

4. Attend every conference and open house.

5. Attend sporting events, plays, and concerts.

Teacher tip:

We really appreciate parents who make an effort to be involved. Sometimes all that's needed is a free box of Kleenex for the classroom. Ask your child's teacher if there's anything they need for the classroom. Shelving unit? Book ends? Folder holders? Used CD player? Maybe there's something in your basement, garage, or attic that could be used.

3: Support the Teacher

Don't defeat the process.

Unbelievably, many parents defeat the whole educational process by undermining the teacher's authority, respect, value and hard work. One thing that nearly all successful students have in common is a parent (or two) who stands behind the teacher.

We teachers talk in the lunchroom, the office, and after school. We all have similar stories and they go something like this:

Jaden and Kylee and Reeves think they don't have to follow the teacher's rules. They flaunt their contempt, telling other students that their parents said they didn't have listen to the teacher.

"My mom said if I need to use the restroom I don't have to wait for a pass, I should just go," one girl said to me in front of the class. The strange thing was that I always handed over the bathroom pass to anyone who asked. Why did she think she needed to announce her rebelliousness and cheeky insubordination to the class?

Students who act defiant or disrespectful claim they don't care about a "citizenship grade" and it's not why they're in school anyway. But it is! Imagine a world where everyone had learned in school how to be good citizens--respectful, not in your face, patient, aware of others' rights. A full education includes learning such important life skills as being on time, doing your work, keeping your mouth shut, asking for permission, and not missing class (work).

When students comes to parent/teacher conferences with their parents and the discussion becomes two (parent and student) against one (the teacher) things rarely work out in favor of the student. It is far better when it's two (parent and teacher) working for one (student). The child may think you're teaming up against him, but positive encouragement and a united front between parent and teacher will lead to much more positive outcomes.

What parents can do to support the teacher:

1. Always attend conferences and open houses.

2. Keep the lines of communication open. Email. Text. Notes.

3. Side with the teacher on behavior and work issues. Support your child in their feelings, but show him that you respect the teachers and their rules first and foremost. (Occasionally there may be personality conflicts between student and teacher, but use that as a learning experience on how to get along with those who rub you the wrong way. It happens in the real world. Learn to deal.)

Teacher tip:

Stress to your child the importance of respecting the

teacher as you would expect to be treated.

4: Curb the Outside Activities

School is like a job.

Remember, your child's job is school. Karate, ballet, soccer, TV, video games, baseball, scouts, etc., are all fine in moderation. Don't let your child get overwhelmed by too many activities.

One or two outside activities should be the norm. Some kids can't even handle one. Some can do three or four, though I'd hope the activities were spread throughout the month and not the week.

Kids need time to daydream. Institute a "quiet time" or

"music time" where they're off the screens and can just think.

Don't let the extra activities replace school. If your child wants to be on a traveling team of some sort that requires them to miss school think twice about letting them try out. There are plenty of teams to join during the summer when school is out.

In the upper grades there are some opportunities that could be considered. Some districts offer internships at jobs or classes at vocational schools that would mean missing part of the school day. That would be fine, but you would be amazed to learn how many teens miss classes regularly in order to babysit or work at a fast food restaurant. Not good. Again, your child's job until they're eighteen is to go to school.

What parents can do:

1. Monitor your child's outside activities.

2. Help your child choose wisely so as not to be overwhelmed.

3. Encourage free time.

4. Attend these activities with the child. (Or spy.)

Teacher tip:

If your child isn't doing as well as he could in class then limit outside of school activities until the report card grades improve.

5: No Jobs

The circular argument doesn't fly.

Don't let your teenager use the car argument: "I need a job to pay for my car." It's a circular argument: why does he need the car? To get to the job. Remember, his job should be school. He will be paid in good grades, a good education and maybe a scholarship (and, by the way, there are many more scholarships for good students than for good athletes).

Of course we're talking here about kids in the upper grades. Maybe their friends have jobs and the extra money is certainly attractive. If it seems so important to them then let them find a summer job, but during the school year their focus should be on school and getting the best grades possible.

One family's oldest daughter did some babysitting, but was not allowed to work a "real job" during the school year. She got good grades and applied for a scholarship at a major university. The money she won paid for four years' worth of tuition, far more money than she would have made (and spent on other things) working at a minimum wage job.

We teachers have had many discussions with students whose grades dropped when they went to work. Their excuses were always, "But I need to work."

When asked why they'd say they needed the money to pay the insurance on their car. "Get rid of the car," we'd say.

"But I need the car to get to work."

It's next to impossible to convince a kid, even as they go deeper into debt and their grades fall, that they should get rid of the car and the job unless a parent steps in and puts their foot down.

What parents can do:

1. Say no to school year jobs.

2. Help them find a summer job that doesn't require them to have a car.

3. Give them an allowance contingent on chores done.

4. Start talking early on about working toward earning a scholarship.

Teacher tip:

Visit the school guidance counselor and get information on current scholarships. There's also plenty of help online.

6 Use Rewards and

Consequences

The carrot and the stick are both

reasonable.

There is nothing wrong with rewarding A's and B's with

money or privileges and there is also nothing wrong with

taking away privileges for unreasonably poor performance.

Sometimes intangible rewards work best. Praise and

respect, more time and attention from you the parent, and even

posting on social media can be more rewarding than money or

gifts.

Learn what motivates your child and use it. Also learn

what consequences they most want to avoid and institute those as well.

What parents can do:

1. Give congratulations, high fives, hugs and kisses.

2. Post A work on the fridge.

3. Call grandparents and brag.

4. Take a special trip or outing.

5. Order something special like pizza or go to an ice cream store.

6. Pay out money for good grades on report cards. Do so directly or open a savings account in the child's name.

7. Extend special privileges (later curfew, sleepover, party, special outing, etc.) for improvement.

8. Take away special privileges for falling grades or failures.

Teacher tip:

If you use monetary rewards make it very clear to your child that school is his job and you are paying him according to his work. Do not delay in handing out rewards. They are most effective if they are immediate, but lose their motivating power if delayed

Having high expectations of your child is great, but make sure they're attainable. Let him know when he's reached or exceeded them.

7: Keep the Teachers

Informed

What do teachers want?

Teachers want all of their students to do well. If there are special circumstances (divorce, death, job loss, health problem, etc.) contact the teacher and explain. I once had a student in class all week and didn't learn until Friday that her mother had been murdered the weekend before.

What parents can do:

1. Contact the school and the individual teacher by phone, text, or email if you're taking your student out of school for several

days. Some teachers will want to send homework first, others will want to wait until he returns.

2. Inform your child's guidance counselor or school social worker if there's a divorce or separation impending or if there's a planned hospital stay.

3. Send a note or make a call if there's a death in the family.

4. Let the teacher know if the family pet is hospitalized or has died. The loss of a pet can be quite traumatic and teachers will make allowances for children who are grieving.

5. Give a heads up if there's an uncommon reason your child must be absent, such as a court summons, a medical test, a college visit, a family member's military deployment, or something else.

Teacher tip:

Know your school's policy on parent-teacher

communication. Some schools, for privacy reasons, may not allow teachers to leave voice mail messages or even send emails. Some schools may have specific methods such as password protected online messaging or fill-in forms. For the most serious conversations use the phone or meet face to face.

8: Don't Cover or Make Excuses for Your Child

Help them learn responsibility.

How will he or she learn to be responsible if you never let them "face the music?"

If you want to know the quickest way to create a spoiled brat, just keep on excusing their behavior. Kids should be held accountable for their behavior, their grades, and who they socialize with. They will have a difficult time in the "real world" where there will be considerable consequences for negative actions, poor work, or bad choices.

What parents can do:

1. Check their homework, but don't do it for them.

2. Help, but don't take over any special projects. Other kids will ridicule someone whose project was obviously done by an adult.

3. Reject stupid excuses, including "I forgot."

4. Love your children, but know that they lie all the time. Really. Kids lie. You know it. Love them, but don't fall for the lies. Stare them down until you get the truth. Raise children who want to tell you the truth.

5. Don't defend them if they've done something wrong. Fold your arms, stand with the teacher (or police) and shake your head. You don't have to answer for them. Let them explain, but again, don't accept a lie.

6. Don't feel sorry for your child if he gets caught doing or saying something he shouldn't have done or said. Shake your head and be quiet. Show your disappointment, but do not cover for your child.

Teacher tip:

We love and respect parents who are objective about their own kids. In the end, it helps your child if you don't try to cover for them, take the blame if their homework is late, or claim they couldn't study for the test because of some excuse you come up with. We teachers can see the difference and are more likely to give a break to a kid who owns up honestly.

9: Pay Attention to What Your Child Wears to School

Common sense isn't common.

Frankly, if it's inappropriate for school, then it's inappropriate. Period.

School uniforms solve so many problems. Unfortunately the vast majority of public schools do not have uniforms and though they may have a dress code, there are countless students, mainly girls, who wiggle their way around the issue.

I once had a male student wear a tee shirt with the most disgusting slogan on it. "Does your mother know you're wearing that to school?" I asked. His reply was that his mother bought it for him on her recent vacation. I had him go to the bathroom and turn it inside out. If I had sent him to the office they would have made more trouble than it was worth and he would have missed more class time.

I also had a female student who consistently wore low cut, cleavage revealing tops. Apparently boob jobs are a fad for teens nowadays, but it's still not appropriate to show cleavage or bellies or butt cracks at school. Double entendre slogans may be cute, but they're distracting in the learning environment.

What parents can do:

1. Go through your child's closet and note what's too tight, too short, too revealing, or has a suggestive slogan. Make it clear that those things are not to be worn to school.

2. If you buy your kid apparel that would raise the eyebrows of a nun or your grandmother please make it crystal clear that said clothing will not be worn to school.

3. Teach your child about fashion and style and what's appropriate for school, funerals, church, weddings, etc. If you don't know, look it up.

Teacher tip:

Go over the student handbook. Please don't let your little girls dress like sluts.

10: Go Over School Rules and Policies Early in the School Year

Be a rule follower.

My husband and I have over 65 years of teaching between the two of us and we know that rules and problems have changed dramatically over the years. Gum chewing, spit wads and pencils in the ceiling are no longer a problem, but water bottles, cell phones, ipods and showing cleavage are.

School policies and rules vary greatly by district. Some schools allow kids to wear ball caps to class, others forbid it (it's an easy way to spot an intruder in the school hallway).

There may or may not be school district rules on cheating, plagiarizing, skipping class, swearing, fighting, bullying and other negative behaviors.

What parents can do:

1. Go over the student conduct guide your school should have provided.

2. Post at home any individual teacher's handout of rules and expectations for their class.

3. Frequently express how disappointed you'd be if your child were to cheat or lie or fail.

Teacher tip:

Teach your child what's acceptable and what's not. It's not as easy as it sounds. Kids will automatically slide into situational ethics if they haven't been raised with a consistent and clear understanding of right and wrong.

11: Talk to Your Kids

Talk it out.

One of the best places for a good talk is in the car where your child is a captive audience, provided the ear buds are out and the phone is off. Also, keep a physical calendar in your house and stay up-to-date on school functions, when to expect progress reports and report cards, and which days your child has off school.

Know who your child's teachers are, what their schedule is, who their friends are, etc.

Once, at parent/teacher conferences, I had a mother express her confusion over how to get her daughter to raise her grades because the girl had no time to study. She was either off with her friends or working. This girl had only a learner's permit, but she was driving the car to work by herself. I told the mom she should take the car keys away and probably have the girl stop working until she was passing all her classes. "I can do that?" the mother asked.

"Of course," I answered, shocked. "It's your car, isn't it? You're the parent. You make the rules."

I still ponder the cluelessness of that parent and how she allowed the child to usurp her authority. And she's not the only one.

What parents can do:

1. Have family time, dinners or game nights or excursions, where you can ask questions.

2. Tell your child what's going on in your life, too. Sometimes talking about your day will encourage your child to confide in you about theirs.

3. Always say goodnight. Bedtime is a great way to spend time with your child. It may last an hour when they're little and

slowly decrease to just a few minutes when they're in high school. But a little time is better than no time. It's a nice routine to finish the day, making sure everyone is offline, off phones, off music, off screens, and ready for bed. Great time to pray with your kid, too.

Teacher tip:

Start conversations wisely. Don't interrogate or drill them about their day. Be casual. Listen more than you talk.

12: Have a Family Night

Together time.

Have a Family Night – or, better yet, go to church together every week. Kids who are taught right from wrong, who hold strong moral beliefs and who are involved with others of strong character stand out from the rest of the student body. Honest.

Research in 2018 showed that families only get 37 minutes a day of quality time together. How are you going to use it? Parenting is the most important role of your life.

What parents can do with their kids:

1. Cook together.

2. Read together

3. Do chores together.

4. Go to the library, grocery store, or gym together.

5. Take a walk together.

6. Play games or sports together.

7. Start a hobby or project together.

8. Go on a mini-vacation.

Teacher tip:

Always, always ask to see your kid's homework. Talk about it. Make sure it gets turned in. Check the backpack regularly.

13: Encourage Reading

Reading.

Reading, reading, reading. Is there anything more important that a kid learns in school? I think not. Everything else is based on the ability to decipher, process, and remember what you read.

What parents can do:

1. Read to your child from infancy.

2. Get your child a library card.

3. Let your child see you enjoying reading.

4. Read the same novels and discuss them.

5. Include a book as a present at Christmas and birthdays.

6. Have your child keep a reading log (or join Goodreads).

7. Go to book stores and used book stores.

8. Set times when everyone in the house reads.

9. Start a book blog with your child to review books they like.

10. Set reading goals.

Teacher tip:

Don't make reading a punishment, make it a privilege and extend the privilege often.

14: Limit Distractions

Distractions, disturbances, and interruptions, oh my.

Distractions are sometimes hard to identify. Yes, phones are a huge distraction so turn them off for family time, reading time, and homework time.

Limit physical clutter in the house. Turn off the TV; there's really very little of actual value on the boob tube.

What parents can do:

1. Prepare a workplace for your child that is clutter free. Set up a spot that will maximize productivity and limit distractions. (So a desk in front of the TV is out.) Whether it's your local

library or just the desk in your bedroom, set aside a study space that your child will want to spend time in. Video game playing should be somewhere else.

2. If your child is going to be working on the computer, set it so the notifications like email and social media are turned off or muted.

3. Close the door and don't interrupt him except to check on progress every 60 to 90 minutes.

Teacher tip:

Kids will swear they work better listening to music, but save the headphones for a reward once the homework is done. A recent university study found that students who studied in complete silence did the best and students who listened to music while studying did the worst.

15: Start a Study Group

Group up.

Having your child meet with classmates who are learning the same things is a good way to go over confusing class material or prepare for a big test. Have them invent quizzes for each other and take turns teaching the material in their own way since teaching someone else is the best way to learn.

This works best in the middle and higher grades, but even kindergartners can get some intrinsic educational value by "playing school" with kids their age.

What parents can do:

1. Encourage your child to find others to work with.

2. Offer your home as a meeting place for a study group.

Teacher tip:

Stay within hear shot and monitor the group without interfering. You can learn a lot about your child and their friends.

16: Ask Questions

What?

Sometimes you, as a parent, won't understand the subject, but that doesn't mean you can't help your student. By asking questions and encouraging your student to teach you the material, your child will focus and learn better.

Take for example a foreign language. Maybe you had Spanish in high school, but your child is learning Japanese. You can help your student by asking him to show you pictures of the words he's learning and repeating the words for you. Have him make a quiz for you. Keep up with this new subject until your child is successful.

What parents can do:

1. Study the textbook yourself and give it a go.

2. Hire a tutor.

3. Have your child try to teach you the material.

4. Ask the teacher for extra help.

Teacher tip:

In most cases a teacher is dealing with too many students and too much paperwork, but I've never known a teacher to refuse to give a kid a little extra time after school. We want our students to be successful. Have your student ask for help.

17: Get Them Involved

Involvement is key.

Encourage your student to get involved in extracurricular activities like sports, clubs, music, dancing, robotics, chess, cooking, tutoring, community work, and church. Enroll in a craft class, try a new sport, help at a soup kitchen, volunteer at the hospital, or read to little kids at the library. A weekly or monthly commitment will help you raise a good person.

You often hear about the "well-rounded" person, meaning they have varied interests and skills. People are unique. You may like one particular sport that your child doesn't even want to give a try. He may be gung-ho for something you're not interested in. I know a dad who was a baseball coach and a train enthusiast. His son tried baseball, but was much more excited about soccer. And as for helping dad with his train layout, forget it. The good thing was that the dad encouraged his son to do what the son liked and didn't make his own disappointment known. Later, when the son was an adult, they bonded over watching football and hockey.

What parents can do:

1. Learn what's available at your child's school. (Sometimes kids don't know all the options, they are only aware of what their closest friends are doing.)

2. Volunteer to help coordinate, coach, or chaperon a particular sport, club, or event.

3. Go with your child to watch, cheer, and sometimes participate in their passions.

Teacher tip:

Don't push your child to stay in an activity that they're really not interested in. Don't push your child to have fun; that kind of pressure doesn't make either of you happy. When they get involved with things they're passionate about they will have fun, they will become dedicated to it, and they will become "well-rounded."

18: Monitor Sleeping Habits

Curfew, anyone?

Set a bedtime or curfew and stick to it. Phones and screens and monitors (and car keys) are under the parents' control. Period. What time does your child need to be up for school? If it's six a.m. then bedtime is nine p.m. End of discussion. Not getting enough sleep affects health and grades, not to mention attitude.

Kids 6 - 13 need 10 - 11 hours of sleep

Kids 14 - 17 need 8 - 10 hours of sleep

What parents can do:

1. Set bedtimes and be consistent

2. Start bedtime routines when they're little.

3. Don't let kids stay up more than an hour later on weekends.

Teacher tip:

When your child insists he needs to stay up an extra hour to study, split the difference and let him study a half hour longer at night and rise a half hour earlier to review.

19: Learn to Say NO

Stop, look, listen, think.

Pause first and give yourself a moment to think about why you're saying NO when your child asks, for example, if they can go watch a hockey match that unfortunately starts at nine p.m. on a school night. Saying NO and backing it up with a precise reason or two will, hopefully, stop the onslaught of begging and nagging. Of course you could surprise your kid with a conditional YES. Yes, you can stay out late this one time, but then I'll expect you to _____ [ace your next test] or [do a particular chore for me] ... you get the picture.

Somewhere along the lines it just becomes easier for some parents to either say no to every request without analyzing it or to give in and say yes to avoid a confrontation or fight. You often hear it said that you need to pick your battles. But why have battles at all? If your child learns that when he asks for something and you say, "Let me think about it" that that's exactly what you'll do, fairly, thoughtfully, and with good reasons. Come back to your child, give your answer, and explain your reasoning. Let them know each request will be considered individually and may not indicate whether you're going to say yes or no or maybe next time.

Example: Mary, a fifth grader, has a new friend who has asked her to a sleepover at her house. Her mother's first reaction is to say no because the friend lives ten miles away, but by saying "Let me think about it" she can come back to Mary and say, "I've thought about it and here's why I'm going to say no this time: I haven't met her parents yet. I don't know anything about the family or how safe it is where they live. Let's invite your friend over here instead for the afternoon and maybe later in the year you can have a sleepover here or there." Isn't that a nicer no?

What parents can do:

Using the "Let me think about it" answer will make it all the more emphatic when you have to say "NO" without the extra time to think about it. Here are the questions that deserve a quick and firm no:

1. Can I go to a friend's house where there won't be any parents? **NO**

2. Can I have a sip of your beer? **NO**

3. I'm not ready for a test, will you let me stay home? **NO**

4. My friends are all going there / doing it / wearing that / saying this, so can I? **NO** (If they have to ask, it's probably something they shouldn't do / wear/ or say.)

5. Can my boyfriend / girlfriend spend the night? **NO**

Teacher tip:

Tell your kids "No, don't take your phone to class."

20: Network

Who's who?

Talk or network with parents of your child's friends and classmates. Present a united front so that everyone agrees that an eight year old's birthday party won't include an R-rated movie, that a day off at the middle school won't mean that a bunch of twelve year olds are congregating at an empty house, or that one stupid parent isn't providing teens with alcohol or renting them a hotel room after the prom.

We could tell you stories. We hear the students talk in the halls, in class, and in the cafeteria because they think we can't hear them. Kids will try to get away with anything. I heard a high school guy tell his friends about how he slipped into his girlfriend's house and spent the night. I discovered a middle schooler's note about a party where all the kids brought cough syrup and pills to experiment with. I was once told by seven year old girl what a blow job was (though she called it a "blue job" and yes, I told her mother what she said).

Of course, other parents are going to have different rules and limitations. Know your child's friends and know their parents. Invite them over. Talk about the serious stuff. It's okay if your child's best friend's father has guns and talks about hunting all the time even if you disapprove or are nervous about having your child around guns. Great conversation starter, right? Talk with the friend's father. Talk with your kid. Don't be judgmental, but make your concerns about safety heard.

If you're the parent with guns in the house, that's fine. You have a right, but remember that others may be uncomfortable or ignorant about hunting or target shooting. Explain your safety measures.

What parents can do:

1. Talk with other parents.

2. Don't be afraid to ask to speak to a friend's parent on the phone.

3. Explain your rules to your child's friends. (Sometimes kids think that when you say "Make yourself at home" that you actually do mean it's okay to raid the fridge or go into the master bedroom or jump on the furniture.)

4. Squeal on kids to their parents if you know something that you'd want to know if it concerned your child: like drugs, drinking, swearing, fighting, cheating, skipping school, etc.

5. Ask other parents what their rules are on things like curfews so when your child says, "But Jimmy's mother lets him stay up until midnight" you can say, "No she doesn't."

Teacher tip:

Get involved in as many school related things as you can, then sit with and talk to the other parents at sports events, plays, concerts, and field trips.

21: Indulge Your Child's Passions

What? They don't have a passion for anything?

Of course they do. You're not looking closely enough. Watch, listen, and learn. Maybe it's something quiet like reading or maybe it's something secret like wishing they could go to space camp, but every kid can get really excited about something. Find out what it is and support them. It'll change next year or maybe even next month. So what? Let them explore life. Life is an adventure.

Tell your child what you loved to do, but don't be disappointed if they have different interests. Give them a chance to experience as many things as they can. Take them to museums. Visit the zoo, the library, the airport, the train station, live theater, the park, the fire station, even a funeral home, or the police station. Take them to watch their friends participate in things. Join a pool, a tennis club, try bowling, mini-golf, or make something (ceramics, sewing, knitting, quilting).

Participating with your child has the added bonus of bringing you closer and creating unforgettable memories.

What parents can do:

1. Start with the library. Check the bulletin board there for ideas.

2. Go online and search out events.

3. Talk with other parents and see what activities, groups, clubs, or sports their children like.

4. Ask your child what he'd like to take classes or lessons in.

Teacher tip:

Rotate out activities, don't keep adding things without subtracting something. Make your child choose only two at a time. Remember, their main thing is to get good grades at school.

22: Help Your Child Set Short Term and Long Term Goals

Goals

Learning how to set realistic goals and how to achieve them is a valuable life-long skill. It promotes a positive attitude, reduces stress, manages procrastination, and sets a good habit.

Goals for small children can be tracked on a worksheet. Maybe it's something simple like making their bed daily.

Goals for older kids might only be discussed or occasionally posted on the fridge for encouragement.

Let them choose their goals. What's something they wish they could achieve? What would they do if they knew they couldn't fail? Discuss the benefits.

Possible goals:

Saving money.

Trying out for and making the team.

Raising their grades.

Reading a certain number of books.

Getting into a particular college.

Developing a specific skill.

Eating healthier foods.

Exercising more.

Giving up a bad habit.

Being on time consistently.

Keeping their bedroom clean.

Perfect attendance.

What parents can do:

1. Brainstorm with your child about how to break a difficult goal into smaller achievable mileposts.

2. Help them plan for potential obstacles including the desire to give up on the goal.

3. Give encouragement and let them know you care about their goals.

Teacher tip: Aim high, but start low.

23: Stay Organized

Use a calendar, an actual physical calendar.

Post it somewhere in your house (kitchen, back door) where everyone can mark down appointments, practices, events, and other reminders. Don't forget to mark down all the parent/teacher open houses and conferences for the whole school year and highlight them. It's a great reminder to kids to see what's coming up and to know that it's important to you to meet with their teachers.

Have your student make his own calendar or notebook in which to keep track of projects, tests, homework, etc. This makes it impossible to forget to do things, study for tests, or bring in supplies.

Of course your child has to look at that calendar or notebook. Create a daily reminder to check it, maybe a post-it note at the door or on the bathroom mirror. Once it becomes a habit, your child will become a more reliable and effective student.

Make sure your student does the homework! The number one surprise I had when I started teaching was to discover how many students did not do the homework. There was a direct impact on grades. One year I had sixty kids in danger of failing. Out of the sixty parents I contacted only three responded to see how they could help. Only three! Parents who used to go to parent-teacher conferences when their child was in first and second grade had somewhere along the line given up their responsibilities. Their teenagers, left to their own devices, went off the rails. **Parents, stay involved!**

What parents can do:

1. Coordinate calendars on phones.

2. Make it a daily habit before everyone is out the door in the morning to check the schedule.

3. Double check that your student has his or her homework done **and turned in.**

Teacher tip:

Sunday is a great day to review the past week and talk about the upcoming one.

24: Study the Report Card

Grades are their paycheck.

Care about your kid's grades!

Even if you got bad grades but turned out just fine I'm sure you'd agree that it wouldn't have hurt if you'd paid a little more attention, studied a little more, or got higher grades. You love your children. You want them to do their best. "Hey, sweetie, go to school and sass the teacher, fail those tests, and let the dog eat your homework," said no parent ever.

If you care about your child's grades so will he. Do you want your kids to do better than you did? I bet you do.

What parents can do:

1. Praise the good grades, give rewards, and talk positively in front of others (friends, grandparents) about what your child is doing well in. Make sure your child overhears that praise.

2. Make a big deal about the A or B or even the C on a difficult test.

3. Put the good stuff on the refrigerator for all to see.

4. Talk to your kid privately about the poor grades and commiserate with him about any failures, but don't punish or belittle the student; he already feels bad.

5. Keep your relationship with your child open and respectful as well as positive.

Teacher tip:

Ask the teacher for help. We care.

25: Don't Make Comparisons

Don't compare your kid to others.

Parents (and teachers) shouldn't compare students with their peers. But of course we do.

Then what happens? There are bound to be inequities. People are different. Students achieve goals at different speeds. Someone is going to be slower, someone is going to be less successful. They can't all be first or all get 100% on everything. Feelings get hurt. Self-esteem withers. Jealousy rises. So does anger.

What parents can do:

1. Don't compare your kid to others, especially a sibling.

2. School is not a competition. Remind your kid of that too. Stress that you want them to do their best.

3. Focus on your child as an individual.

4. Help your children figure out what they can do to make themselves better.

Teacher tip:

Follow up after parent/teacher conferences and ask if your child is doing better.

26: Avoid Procrastination

Avoid procrastination at all costs.

This is probably the #1 curse of all students. Occasionally, they can let something slide, but when big tests, exams, and essays come, your child must be prepared. You'll both be sorry in the end, (especially later in college when they'll have to write long papers or do hefty amounts of reading).

When I assigned something humongous like a research paper or a project that would take several hours at home to complete I made sure to have several pre-deadline checkpoints. Not all teachers do this, but when your child gets a big assignment sit down with him and figure out a timeline of work so the entire project is more manageable. Divide it up into several deadlines of shorter chunks and make that final deadline earlier than the teacher wants by a couple of days.

What parents can do:

1. Monitor your child and help him get accustomed to getting things done early and out of the way rather than waiting until the very last minute.

2. Make a plan and a list of homework. Keep it somewhere you both can see it and won't forget it.

3. Stress to your child that "Due dates" are really "Do before" dates.

Teacher tip:

Don't ask the teacher for an extension unless your child has been in the hospital or home sick for an extended period of time.

27: Track Nutrition

It's your responsibility.

As a parent you are responsible to make sure your child eats breakfast and lunch. Sounds obvious, but you'd be surprised how many parents don't know that their kid skips breakfast or lunch. Grab and go food is fine: apples, bananas, granola bars, peanut butter crackers, hard boiled eggs, etc.

Hungry students don't pay attention. Lunch is important too. Make a bag lunch the night before or give them lunch money.

In our home we used to give them lunch money every week to cover three days' worth of lunches. They had to make their lunch for the other two days. It was interesting to see who would opt to make more lunches and save the cash. A lot of lessons were learned that way.

What parents can do:

1. Have a good supply of grab and go items like breakfast bars and fruit.

2. Encourage them to make their own or help you make the next day's brown bag lunch.

3. Talk about the importance of not skipping meals.

4. Limit those unhealthy snacks like chips and sugary drinks.

Teacher tip:

The number of kids with severe life-threatening allergies to foods like peanuts is on the rise. Are you and your child aware of your school's rules and/or efforts to protect these kids? Have a serious talk with your child about not teasing these kids and definitely not tempting them to eat something forbidden.

28: Who? What's His Name?

Know your child's friends and their parents.

Know where they live and don't let your child go to their house unless you've been inside yourself. Really? Is this necessary? Yup. Do they have guns and are they locked up? Do they have alcohol and is it locked up? Do they have internet or cable and are there parental controls to block the porn? Tell me, who is more important in this world than your child? Be vigilant, be protective, be a parent.

We sat our oldest down when she entered eighth grade to have a serious talk. She'd made a friend with a girl who we could see would only be trouble for her (we'd already dealt with literally thousands of teenagers and knew the signs well enough). We talked frankly and predicted that this friend would get pregnant and drop out of school. We did not forbid the friendship, but put restrictions on it such as the friend could come to our house where there was always an adult around, but our daughter could not go to her place where there wasn't. We encouraged our kid to be a good friend and to be a good example and make intelligent choices. Long story short: when our prediction came true we had another talk. Yes, we said "We told you so." Years later, as a single mom, the friend reconnected with our daughter and confessed that she wished she'd had a family like ours.

No matter how vigilant you are things will happen. You may go to a graduation party and be seated across from a couple of kids who haven't yet been caught for the car-jacking, abduction and murder of a young woman. That happened to us. Our daughter was friends with a girl whose cousin was one of the murderers. Sometimes there's nothing you can do to protect your child from certain circumstances.

What parents can do:

1. Have your child's friends' names and phone numbers.

2. Know where your kid is going and who they're hanging out with.

3. Make a pact with your child that they will call you if they're in an uncomfortable situation.

Teacher tip:

Ask the teacher if they see any signs that your child may be in an unhealthy friendship.

29: Be Wise

Share your wisdom with your child.

When you run out of your own wise words here are some more:

Always use sunscreen.

Take notes in class.

Review your notes daily.

If you can't say anything nice about someone, don't say anything at all.

Wash out your water bottle with soap and hot water.

Keep a breath mint or gum in your pocket.

Practice things in front of the mirror.

Don't put anything online that you wouldn't want your

parents, grandparents, or future spouse to see.

Sit up straight in class, you'll learn more (really, this works).

If you believe you can become smarter, you will.

Don't label yourself negatively.

What parents can do:

1. What worked for you? Tell your kid.

2. What mistakes did you make in school? Own up to them and tell them to learn from your errors.

3. What embarrassing things happened to you? These are things you don't want to happen to your child, right? So why not tell them your stories?

4. What tips would you pass on? Make a list and share them casually.

Teacher tip:

Always greet your teacher when you enter a classroom. Always say goodbye to your teacher when you leave (this causes borderline grades to be rounded up favorably, really).

30: Exercise

Exercise!

Exercise regularly. Walk the dog. Walk with mom. Go to the gym. Join a sport. Start a neighborhood ball game. Read a book on a stationary bike. Something, anything, just get moving. Shopping counts.

Sitting around staring at a screen might be learning or socializing, but please help your child learn some skills like playing catch, hopping, jumping, skipping, and swimming.

What parents can do:

1. Lead by example. Be active. Join in their games.

2. Keep an exercise calendar when they're little and make

exercise and play a habit. Good health is its own reward.

3. Insist on 15 minutes of exercise for every hour of screen time.

4. Provide active toys and games.

5. Choose activities that are developmentally appropriate.

6. Use physical activity as a reward. Your child will love 20 minutes of shooting hoops with you as a break from homework.

7. Make exercise a non-negotiable routine, just like wearing a seat belt, brushing their teeth, or showering daily.

8. Put your kid in charge of your physical activity. It'll be fun.

Teacher tip:

Don't make your kid run laps or do push-ups as a punishment.

31: Manage Stress

Even little kids feel stress.

With bigger kids there are bigger stresses as the hormones kick in.

Life can be frustrating as you're learning who you are, where you fit in, what you're good at, what makes you happy, and what (and who) annoys you.

Tests and quizzes, even homework, can stress a kid out. And then there's the social stuff. *Does he or she like me? Was I left out on purpose? Who said what about me?*

You don't have to yell at your kid for them to think you're yelling at them. That's just common kid talk: "My mom yelled at me last night to clean my room" when all you did was say in a calm and quiet voice, "This room is a mess. Why don't you clean it up?"

Understand that growing up (especially going through the teen years) is inherently stressful. Watch for the signs that stress is getting to your child. Signs show up as anxiety, snippiness, nail-biting, knuckle-cracking, sudden crying, unexplained outbursts, withdrawal from family or friends, or other sudden and unusual behaviors.

What parents can do:

1. Take time to relax with your kid.

2. Play a game.

3. Take a walk with them.

4. Read together. It will relax you both.

5. Cook together.

6. Clean their room with them. What? Trust me, kids can get

stressed out because their space is disorderly. Help them clear more space and have a better (safer) environment where they won't trip over toys or lose their homework assignments.

7. Pray together.

Teacher tip:

Unplug the headphones and have your child listen to instrumental music at lower decibels.

32: Study Smart

Use memory techniques.

Encourage your student to use memory techniques when studying. There are lots of tricks and you and your child can learn them.

Acronyms and acrostics are helpful. Need to remember the five Great Lakes? Just think HOMES. Each letter stands for a lake: Huron, Ontario, Michigan, Erie, and Superior

Here's an example of using an acrostic to remember the order of the planets:

My Very Excited Mother Just Served Us Nuts

Mercury Venus Earth Mars Jupiter Saturn Uranus

Neptune

Using acronyms and acrostics is a type of association. There are other types of associations. I could never remember if port or starboard was the left side of the ship until I made the association of port and left both having four letters.

Need to learn a grocery list of words? Think of five rooms in your house and five places in each room. That gives you twenty five places to work with. If I had to remember to get lettuce, jelly, tortilla shells, olives, vitamins, and twenty other things I might start with the kitchen and imagine the lettuce on the stove (one of my five spots in the kitchen). I imagine that the lettuce is melting onto the burner and I'll never get it scraped off, the jelly is smeared all over the front of refrigerator where it's sliming down onto the floor that I'll have to clean; there are tortilla shells wrapped around the faucets in the sink, holding back the water; black olives are dancing in a line inside the microwave, throwing themselves against the glass; and in spot number five, the kitchen table, my vitamins are spilling out on the placemats, forming words that are not complimentary. I do this with the rest of my list and when I get to the store I just visualize my kitchen and remember what was in those five places--olives in the microwave, jelly on the fridge--and continue on with however many rooms and items I need. Of course, I could just write a grocery list, but the point is your student may have to memorize a list of some kind and this method is great for short term memory challenges. If you include some emotional connection (like thinking I'll burn my fingers scraping the lettuce off the stove or being humiliated by what the vitamins spell out about me) then the connections last longer.

How would you use this technique for school if you had to learn the order of the U.S. presidents? Easy. Assign a president to each place in your house. There's President Washington at your stove jamming a cherry tree into the oven and clacking his wooden teeth at you. Next imagine John Adams at your fridge, grabbing an apple out of the fruit bin and hitting himself with it on his Adam's apple. Get it? That will help you remember that the second president was Adams. Your third spot was the sink and there, soaking his rear end in it is

Jefferson, pointing his finger at you and waving the Declaration of Independence. And so on. This can be a lot of fun if you work this out with your child.

Another memory technique is music. Lyrics, that often rhyme, are helpful prompts. Using tunes you already know makes it easy. And then there's rap music. Believe it or not coming up with a rap about something is an effective memory skill.

Recording yourself repeating the answers to whatever you're learning is another helpful strategy. Using a different voice or accent can make it fun. Then listen back several times and re-record without the script. See how well you do.

One of the very best ways to learn is to teach. How would you explain this math problem or that Spanish grammar rule or the plot of your English novel if you were the teacher? Enlist a parent or sibling as your student, but prepare first before making your presentation. Use visuals, computer, or whatever and test your "student" afterward.

What parents can do:

1. Buy a book on memory tricks and go over it with your child.

2. Study with your child.

3. Be a student for your child to teach something to. Let him quiz you, too.

Teacher tip:

Repetition is the key to learning.

33: Mistakes are Good

Learn from your mistakes.

We learn best from our mistakes, starting with burning a finger on a hot stove. Some people seem to think that mistakes should be avoided at all costs, but I say it's a smart person who can learn from their mistakes and a wise person who can learn from others' mistakes.

What parents can do:

1. Have your child go through every mistake he makes in tests and exams. He needs to analyze why he made each mistake. Was it carelessness, forgetfulness, poor understanding, plain old stupidity? Oops. Go ahead and groan with him at his

failures, allow him to feel silly or foolish or humiliated or angry. Tell him to use those emotions to help him learn.

2. Find out what the right answers are and help your kid study them. He won't want to feel those negative emotions next time.

3. Incorporate practice tests.

Teacher tip:

Make test-taking less stressful by telling your children from the time they start school that you view tests as exciting and fun.

34: School Attendance

Remember, school is their job.

Make attendance at school a priority. This goes for parents too. Don't miss open houses, conferences, or other activities. Don't take your kids out of school for a week for a vacation that fits your schedule. There are twelve other weeks when the kid's not in school. Limit sick days, too. Sure, keep him home if he's really sick, vomiting, infectious, or feverish, but no kid needs a "personal" day. That's what Saturday and Sunday are for. If they can't achieve perfect attendance at least keep the absences to a minimum of three or four for the year. **Every day in school is important.**

What parents can do:

1. Don't give in to frivolous reasons for missing school.

2. Remind kids how hard it is to make up work, and how it'll pile up, if they miss too often.

3. Don't forget to monitor bedtime. There's no good reason to stay up past 9 p.m.

Teacher tip:

A parent who contributes to a child's truancy from school can be charged with a misdemeanor.

Final tip:

Be there. The most important thing to be successful in school is for your kid to **be there** and for you to **be there** for your kid.

35: Other Books

We sincerely hope that this has been of some value to you. If so, a positive review on Amazon would be greatly appreciated.

Other books by Debra Chapoton include:

Fiction:

THE GIRL IN THE TIME MACHINE A desperate teen with a faulty time machine. What could go wrong? 17-year-old Laken is torn between revenge and righting a wrong. SciFi suspense.

THE TIME BENDER A stolen kiss could put the universe at risk. Selina doesn't think Marcum's spaceship is anything more than one heck of a science project ... until he takes her to the moon and back.

THE TIME PACER Alex discovered he was half-alien

right after he learned how to manipulate time. Now he has to fight the star cannibals, fly a space ship, work on his relationship with Selina, and stay clear of Coreg, full-blooded alien rival and possible galactic traitor. Once they reach their ancestral planet all three are plunged into a society where schooling is more than indoctrination

THE TIME STOPPER Young recruit Marcum learns battle-craft, infiltration and multiple languages at the Interstellar Combat Academy. He and his arch rival Coreg jeopardize their futures by exceeding the space travel limits and flying to Earth in search of a time-bender. They find Selina whose ability to slow the passage of time will be invaluable in fighting other aliens. But Marcum loses his heart to her and when Coreg takes her twenty light years away he remains on Earth in order to develop a far greater talent than time-bending. Now he's ready to return home and get the girl.

THE TIME ENDER Selina Langston is confused about recurring feelings for the wrong guy/alien. She's pretty sure Alex is her soulmate and Coreg should not be trusted at all. But

Marcum ... well, when he returns to Klaqin and rescues her she begins to see him in a different light.

EDGE OF ESCAPE Innocent adoration escalates to stalking and abduction in this psychological thriller. Also available in German, titled SOMMERFALLE.

THE GUARDIAN'S DIARY Jedidiah, a 17-year-old champion skateboarder with a defect he's been hiding all of his life, must risk exposure to rescue a girl that's gone missing.

SHELTERED Ben, a high school junior, has found a unique way to help homeless teens, but he must first bring the group together to fight against supernatural forces.

A SOUL'S KISS When a tragic accident leaves Jessica comatose, her spirit escapes her body. Navigating a supernatural realm is tough, but being half dead has its advantages. Like getting into people's thoughts. Like taking over someone's body. Like experiencing romance on a whole new plane - literally.

EXODIA By 2093 American life is a strange mix of failing technologies, psychic predictions, and radiation induced abilities. Tattoos are mandatory to differentiate two classes, privileged and slave. Dalton Battista fears that his fading tattoo is a deadly omen. He's either the heir of the brutal tyrant of the new capital city, Exodia, or he's its prophesied redeemer.

OUT OF EXODIA In this sequel to EXODIA, Dalton Battista takes on his prophesied identity as Bram O'Shea. When this psychic teen leads a city of 21st century American survivalists out from under an oppressive regime, he puts the escape plan at risk by trusting the mysterious god-like David Ronel.

Children's Books:

THE SECRET IN THE HIDDEN CAVE 12-year-old Missy Stark and her new friend Kevin Jackson discover dangerous secrets when they explore the old lodge, the woods, the cemetery, and the dark caves beneath the lake. They must solve the riddles and follow the clues to save the old lodge from destruction.

MYSTERY'S GRAVE After Missy and Kevin solved THE SECRET IN THE HIDDEN CAVE, they thought the rest of the summer at Big Pine Lodge would be normal. But there are plenty of surprises awaiting them in the woods, the caves, the stables, the attic and the cemetery. Two new families arrive and one family isn't human.

BULLIES AND BEARS In their latest adventure at Big Pine Lodge, Missy and Kevin discover more secrets in the caves, the attic, the cemetery and the settlers' ruins. They have to stay one step ahead of four teenage bullies, too, as well as three hungry bears. This summer's escapades become more and more challenging for these two twelve-year-olds. How will they make it through another week?

A TICK IN TIME 12-year-old Tommy MacArthur plunges into another dimension thanks to a magical grandfather clock. Now he must find his way through a strange land, avoid the danger lurking around every corner, and get back home. When he succeeds he dares his new friend Noelle to return with him, but who and what follows them back means more trouble and more adventure.

BIGFOOT DAY, NINJA NIGHT When 12-year-old

Anna skips the school fair to explore the woods with Callie, Sydney, Austin, and Natalie, they find evidence of Bigfoot. No way! It looks like his tracks are following them. But that's not the worst part. And neither is stumbling upon Bigfoot's shelter. The worst part is they get separated and now they can't find Callie or the path that leads back to the school.

In the second story Luke and his brother, Nick, go on a boys only camping trip, but things get weird and scary very quickly. Is there a ninja in the woods with them? Mysterious things happen as day turns into night.

Non-fiction:

HOW TO BLEND FAMILIES A guide for stepparents

BUILDING BIG PINE LODGE A journal of our experiences building a full log home

CROSSING THE SCRIPTURES A Bible Study supplement for studying each of the 66 books of the Old and New Testaments.

Made in the USA
Monee, IL
25 March 2021

63781966R00059